Watermelon Seeds

Watermelon Seeds

Shelby C. Bacus

Oso good publications

Copyright © 2024 by Shelby C. Bacus

All rights reserved. No part of this book may be reproduced in any manner whatsoever without written permission except in the case of brief quotations embodied in critical articles and reviews.

First Printing, 2024

Be kind always.

Table of contents
1 Cognitive dissonance
2 Sweet death
3 Come become
4 Crowded table
5 Action
6 Changing perspective
7 Entirely
8 Just was
9 Sleep talk
10 Lip prints
11 Trust
12 Define
13 Grey area
14 Found
15 Risk
16 Haunted house
17 Everything
18 Spelling bee
19 Hurt people
20 Heartbeat
21 Shooting star
22 Full
23 Lifelines
24 Bitter
25 Breath
26 Pond
27 Dreaming of you
28 Miscommunication

29 Night owl
30 Watermelon seeds
31 Circular
32 Stayed
33 The right track
34 Always here
35 Punchline
36 Night and day
37 180
38 Release
39 Apology
40 Music box
41 Aware
42 Tidal
43 Forget
44 Scales
45 Heart
46 Forever
47 Moon
48 Big
49 Kitchen cabinets
50 Sandpaper
51 Solstice
52 Winter sun
53 Incandescent
54 Change of perspective
55 Ghost town
56 Past life
57 Pierce

58 Muse
59 Tongue twister
60 Velcro
61 Nightlight
62 Eclipse
63 (Live)strong
64 Red giant
65 Drowning
66 Wonders
67 Vinyl
68 Tick tock
69 Stepping stool
70 Meandering
71 Scratched record
72 Flipside
73 Insomnia
74 Nostalgia
75 Jelly beans
76 Missed connections
77 Cultivate
78 Flips
79 Bruise
80 Heavy Sighs
81 Sun rises
82 River
83 Overflow
84 Mundanity
85 Testing the waters
86 Silence

87 Dream girl
88 Frozen
89 Nuance
90 Post grad
91 Seen
92 Thrift store guitar
93 Downpour
94 Mockingbird
95 Windows
96 Power lines
97 Oversaturated
98 Less
99 Simple things
100 Too much
101 Patches
102 Sea glass
103 Confessional
104 Weeds
105 Little details
106 Enlightenment
107 Cold feet
108 Caught in your arms

<u>Cognitive dissonance</u>
I always thought that my biggest barrier
To being vulnerable was my fear of
Being judged by others.
However, I think what I fear more
Is actually my own self judgement.
Being vulnerable, means opening myself
Up to others, but also opening myself
Up to my myself.
Being vulnerable, means having to not only
Confront, but relive my own shame, guilt,
Regret, grief, disappointment, fear, dread,
Worry, anxiety, loneliness and sadness.
All of which I have neatly compartmentalized
And set aside, to deal with at a later time.
Being vulnerable, forces me to confront these
Feelings- the thought of which is terrifying.
I am, after all, my own harshest critic.
Cognitive dissonance is believing that when
Other people are vulnerable, they are
Courageous; but when I am vulnerable,
I am weak.
How do I show myself the same empathy
That I would show anyone else?

Self love.
Self acceptance.
Self forgiveness.
/easier said than done/a work in progress/

<u>Sweet death</u>
Flowers growing in cemeteries
Are just the dead pushing their
Good back into the world

Where bees spread the
Messages of the dead
Pollinating flower after flower

Reminding the living
That sometimes death
Turns into honey.

<u>Come become</u>
Come to me as you are,
Wherever you are.
Root yourself here.
There is room in
This garden for you
To grow freely and
Unhindered.

Come become.

<u>Crowded table</u>
My love language is
Cooking for other people
While the perfect Spotify
Playlist is gently playing
In the background.

Happiness, is a
Crowded kitchen table.

<u>Action</u>
Someone can say they
Love you but still be unkind.
It is not enough to just
Profess your love.
Love is an action
Not an affirmation.

<u>Changing perspective</u>
It is not until now that
I'm beginning to realize
That the kind of love
That I want, is not
The kind of love
I have known.

<u>Entirely</u>
When I first came out to you
I was grateful that you still
Wanted to be apart of my life.
The reality being, you didn't
Want to be apart of my entire life.

I've noticed when we talk -
You never ask me about her.
My entirety.
Her.
Entirely.

<u>Just was</u>
There's a story in the bible
Where Moses asked God
To reveal Their face to him
But God said that if Moses were
To look Them in the face
He would be too overwhelmed and die.
Instead, God revealed to Moses
Where They had just been.

Looking at you, is like looking
At where God just was.

<u>Sleep talk</u>
You sleep talk
In a language
I don't understand.
I try learning it
So I can understand
Your dreams.

<u>Lip prints</u>
Your wine glass from last night
Still sits in my dishwater.
Unable to wash away
What's left of you.
Your lips printed on the rim.
Imprinted on my mind-
On my body.

<u>Trust</u>
People won't ever
Prove you wrong
Until you give them
A chance to.

<u>Define</u>
The way we define
Love, determines how
We experience it.

<u>Grey area</u>

Do you ever feel like
You've fallen somewhere
In between lives?
Somewhere between your
Past self, present self, and future self?
Unable to jump into the periphery?

<u>Found</u>
I'm not the same person
From years ago.
That person was lost.
And although I still
Don't know where
I'm going, I've found
Where I am.

<u>Risk</u>
Take the risk.
It is better to feel
Pain than regret.

<u>Haunted house</u>
The joy this house once gave me
Left when you left, but I still find myself
Sleeping on my side of the bed
Making space for you.

The memories woven into
The foundation of this home
Haunt me like a
Conscious nightmare.

I hope that as I box this place up
I can also box you up, but I know
Not even a storage unit can
Keep you out of my mind.

You engraved yourself into me-
And while the scar of you will heal
With time, the memory of you
Will never fade.

<u>Everything</u>
To fully love someone
Is to let them see every part
Of what has made you, you.

Spelling bee
Attractiveness is often
Spelled "b-e-i-n-g-k-i-n-d"

<u>Hurt people</u>
I choose to believe that
Every rude person is going
Through something unimaginable.
Because sometimes hurt people
Hurt people. But kind people
Help heal hurt people.

<u>Heartbeat</u>
The first time I fell
In love with you
You were dancing
In the driveway
With earbuds in.
I knew in that moment
That I would spend
The rest of my life
Trying to figure out
Which song beats
To the same rhythm
As your heart.

<u>Shooting star</u>
You caught me in
Your gravity but I
Burned up before
I reached you.

<u>Full</u>
Every day I spend with you
Is another stretch mark
Left on my heart.

<u>Lifelines</u>
In the end, I hope
My life is measured
In the amount of
Laugh lines that
Wrinkle my face.

<u>Bitter</u>
Even covered in honey
You still taste bitter.

<u>Breath</u>
In the stillness of a
Cold winter morning
Our souls reveal a
Bit of themselves
With every exhalation
Of our lungs -
No matter how brief.

<u>Pond</u>
You are a frozen pond
In which I am able to see
Into, but am unable to
Break through.

<u>Dreaming of you</u>
You're gone but
I still talk to you
In my sleep.

<u>Miscommunication</u>
In my inability to
Convey to you my
Own unhappiness
I never gave you
The opportunity to
Do things differently.

<u>Night Owl</u>
When the sun goes down
I shed the shadows that
Drag alongside me-
Free at last.

<u>Watermelon seeds</u>
When you look at me,
My stomach flutters.
As if all the watermelon seeds
I swallowed as a kid
Were sprouting simultaneously
Within me.

<u>Circular</u>

Nourish what nourishes
Your soul. Feed what
Feeds you. Water what
Waters you. Give to that
Which gives to you.

<u>Stayed</u>
I often spend too much
Time dwelling on those
Who left. Those that left
Simply because they
Wanted to. However,
I want to spend more
Time focusing on the
People who stayed.
Because even though
People have come and
Gone from my life-
The right people
Always stayed.

<u>The right track</u>
When we fall off track,
It's sometimes better
To get on a new one,
Instead of getting back
On the same track
We keep falling off of.

<u>Always here</u>
There are days in which
I need to remember that
It is ok to run into my own
Arms, instead of theirs.

<u>Punchline</u>
I love the way you start
Laughing at your own
Joke before you get to
Telling it. If it keeps you
Laughing, I hope we never
Get to the punchline.

<u>Night and day</u>
Falling in love with you
Is like the night falling
In love with the day.
Always chasing,
Never catching.

<u>180</u>
Like many, I developed
Anxiety later in life. But,
There are some days that
I wonder, if maybe I've had
Anxiety my entire life. And
What originally manifested
As anticipation and excitement,
Later turned to worry and dread.
As if my mind tricked itself into
Taking something positive and
Turning the chemicals in my
Brain into something negative.

Release

My heart was infected
With so much distrust
That I couldn't even
Tell my therapist my
Deepest truths.
It wasn't that I had
Anything of particular
Interest to hide, but I'd
Gone through life only
Giving out my trust
To those who had
Given me theirs.
It's taken me a long
Time, but I'm finally
At a place where I
Feel as though I can
Place my trust in
Others before they
Necessarily put their
Trust in me.

<u>Apology</u>
If there are those out there
That I've hurt and not realized it,
I am sorry.

<u>Music box</u>
A carved wooden woman
Trapped inside the confines
Of a (man)made, Four-
Walled prison.
Bent over, lying in wait
For another hand to wind
Her up, commanding her
To dance.

<u>Aware</u>
I don't think I was ever
Aware that I was living,
Until I first felt pain.

As if it first takes pain
For us to realize
What is at stake.

<u>Tidal</u>
I'm tired of the highs and
Lows associated with
Being in your orbit. The
Way you pull me in then
Push me away with
Concerning ease.
I'd rather sever ties
With the moon, than
Continue this
Exhausting
Cycle.

<u>Forget</u>
There are days that I wish
We had never met. Only
So that I can feel what
It was like meeting you
For the first time again.

<u>Scales</u>
I hope one day you can
Trust me enough to shed
The scales that you covered
Your heart in.

<u>Heart</u>
When the doctors
Tried to measure
Your heart, you
Broke their
Scale.

<u>Forever</u>
After meeting you,
I hope we never
Become strangers.

<u>Moon</u>
Your presence
Moves oceans.

<u>Big</u>
The transplant surgeons
Didn't know what to do
With your heart when
They saw it. Surely no
One would be capable
Of receiving a heart
So big.

<u>Kitchen cabinets</u>
There are cabinets in my kitchen
That I hardly ever open. Cabinets
That probably haven't been opened
Since I first unpacked the place.

However, there are some cabinets
That I open every day. The cabinets
That hold my spices, plates, bowls,
And all of my coffee mugs.

Even so, I still haven't found a
Favorite coffee mug of mine,
Or the whisk that my mother once
Gave me, since moving in.

But one day, when I first started
Going to therapy, my therapist told
Me that I couldn't selectively numb
My emotions. That when

I numb the negative emotions
I also numb the positive ones.
That without letting myself feel
Grief or anger or fear

SHELBY C. BACUS

    I would never feel the comfort
    Of joy or pride or gratefulness. Just
    Dimly lit emotions packed away in
    Forgotten kitchen cabinets.

    The day that I finally decided to
    Open one of those forgotten
    Kitchen cabinets, is also the day
    That I found everything that I had

    Thought I lost.

<u>Sandpaper</u>
Your embrace can
Smooth over even
My roughest surfaces.

<u>Solstice</u>
After the darkest
Day of the year,
The light starts
To return.

<u>Winter sun</u>
I told the sun it was
December so she took
Her light and left-
Taking my light
With her.

<u>Incandescent</u>
The way the winter sun
Shines through the trees
Can never be recreated.

<u>Change of perspective</u>
My worries began to
Tower over me so I
Bought a plane ticket
Hoping my fears would
Appear smaller from
The sky.

<u>Ghost town</u>
Even in a city of hundreds
Of thousands of people,
I still fear that I'm going
To run into you.

<u>Past life</u>
Are my memories still mine
Even if I don't want them?

<u>Pierce</u>
Is it painful when the
Sun pierces through
The clouds?

<u>Muse</u>
If you think one of
My poems was
Written about you,
It probably was.

<u>Tongue twister</u>
In school we used to
Practice tongue twisters.
Phrases that were
Designed to be difficult
To articulate properly.
But when we grew up
No one told us that the
Most difficult tongue twister
To say would be
"I love you".

<u>Velcro</u>

You tore my heart away
When you left, and the
Whole world heard
Us come apart.

<u>Nightlight</u>
I admire your ability
To shine through
The darkness.

<u>Eclipse</u>
Your presence in a room
Is so inflated that you
Obstruct the light of
Others trying to shine
Through.

<u>(Live)strong</u>
There was a time growing up that
Wearing a circular piece of
Yellow rubber around your wrist,
Was the peak of fashion.
That little piece of rubber
Proclaiming to "livestrong."
The irony being that when
My friend decided to take
His own life in high school,
We were given the same rubber
Bracelets in his memory, but
Instead of telling us to "livestrong"
We were told to "always remember."

<u>Red giant</u>
Your so(u)l shines as bright
As the sun. Engulfing everything
Around you in light and warmth.
And when your soul nears its end
It will only to continue to expand
Outwards, touching every so(u)l in
Its orbit.

<u>Drowning</u>
I'm drowning in your eyes
And I have no desire to
Take a breath.

<u>Wonders</u>
The best gift you ever gave me,
Was being able to discover the
Greatest wonders of this world
For a second time through your eyes.

<u>Vinyl</u>
There is nothing more romantic
Than when someone decides
To play music for you on
A record player.

Record players require
Commitment and constant
Involvement, with albums being
Chosen with purpose & intent.

A brave move to make
In a universe where playlists
Can simply be auto generated
For any mood, moment, or person.

But I think you can learn a lot
About someone based off
Of the records they decide
To share with you.

More importantly, I think you
Can learn a lot about yourself
Based off the music they decide
To share with you.

The rotating vinyl a
Reflection of yourself
In the eyes and ears
Of another.

<u>Tick tock</u>

When my eyes flutter open in the morning
I am immediately hit with the overwhelming
Sensation that I'm running out of time.
Running out of time to accomplish, to succeed,
To push forward. Running out of time to be.
But when my eyes focus on you laying
Beside me, the ticking clock in my head quiets.

There's no such thing as wasting time
When I'm with you.

<u>Stepping stool</u>
You watched the wood bend against your will,
And you still wonder why the stepping stool
Broke beneath your feet; when every time
You used it, it weakened underneath.

<u>Meandering</u>
Sometimes I feel as though I
Am just a river looking for an
Ocean.

<u>Scratched record</u>
My favorite record is imperfectly perfect.
There's a large scratch on the vinyl that makes
A verse from a song repeat a few times before
It moves forward. It gets stuck on the line
"We love our lovin", as if it knows we need to
Hear it a few times before we can comprehend it.

<u>Flipside</u>

Getting to know someone
Is like listening to vinyl-
You have to listen to the
Flipside in order to hear
The entire album.
Yet, how often do people
Actually take the time to
Listen to the B side of a
Record? Think about all
Vinyl currently left forgotten
In record players. Where do
You think the dust settles?

Only on the A side.

Insomnia
Grab my hand and leap
Off this cliff with me.
If you can't fall asleep
On your own, we'll
Fall together.

<u>Nostalgia</u>
Moments of immense
Longing for a past life;
Until I met you.

Now there is no
Sentimentality for my
Life before you.

<u>Jelly beans</u>
You picked out your favorites
And threw the rest in the trash.

<u>Missed connections</u>
To the cute girl at the bus stop
Who gave me the book out of her
Hands when I had mentioned I'd been
Wanting to read it for ages; even though
You hadn't had a chance to finish it yet-
Reach out to me, because I think this
Story has a happy ending that you're
Going to want to be a part of.

<u>Cultivate</u>
My soul was rotting so
I took a plow to my heart
To try and prepare it to
Receive a seed and grow
Into something living.

<u>Flips</u>
My body is in a
Constant narrative
With itself always
Telling my heart
To do a flip.

<u>Bruise</u>
A visual symbol that
Silently allows others
To know that we've been
Hurt, but we're healing.

If only people could see
When our hearts or
Our minds have been hurt,
But we are healing.

<u>Heavy sighs</u>
An audible release of
Something you can
No longer keep inside.

<u>Sun rises</u>
To be as selfless as
The sun who rises
No matter if there
Is anyone to watch
Her do it.

<u>River</u>
If time is a river,
I'll build a dam
To stop it from
Flowing so that
I can make each
And every moment
With you last.

<u>Overflow</u>
I built a dam to stop
The river of time,
But the dam burst
And my life flashed
Before my eyes.

Mundanity

When our minds are not occupied
By the constant stimulation of new
Experiences or environments, there
Is nothing to distract ourselves from
The constant passing of time.

That's why our childhoods lasted
For what seemed like forever.
Everyday we were exposed to
Something extraordinary that distracted
Our minds from time passing.

As adults, how can we capture
That same state of wonder & naivety?
How can we escape the mundanity
Of our lives, and divert focus onto
Anything but our obsession with time?

Testing the waters
The sun's been dipping
Her toes in the pool
To see if she's ready to
Come back in full force.

<u>Silence</u>
My soul screams out to you
Telling you to run, but only
Silence leaves my mouth,
Begging you to stay.

<u>Dream girl</u>
The hardest part of waking up
Is realizing that you are no
Longer laying next to me.

<u>Frozen</u>
When I went to hold your heart
I was burned by it's coldness.

Nuance

I love that I can tell what mood you're in based on the color of your coffee.
I love that I can tell when you're mad at me when you text me a :) instead of an emoji.
I love that I can tell when you are anxious when you start organizing our pantry.
I love that I can tell when you're texting your parents based on the repetitive sighs escaping from your mouth.

But most of all, I love that I can always tell that you love me, because you make it a point to never let it be a question.

<u>Post grad</u>
Nearing the end of something that you've
Spent the past five years trying to accomplish
Is a feeling riddled with conflicting emotions.

Excitement; you did that damn thing.
Dread; what's the next damn thing I have to do?

Gratefulness; all the hard work has paid off.
Resentment; I had to make many sacrifices.

Hope; what's in store for me next?
Fear; what's in store for me next?

What is in store for me next?
The effect of these feelings are nuanced by any
Given day, and by those who I surround myself
With. And while the future may be unclear, it's
Comforting to know that I've made it through
The past five years.

<u>Seen</u>
Attentiveness and perceptiveness
Are probably the most intimate
Expressions of love.

<u>Thrift store guitar</u>
I often wonder about how
Many hands have held you,
And the music that they created.

You were a thrift store find
That ended up saving my life.
A therapy I desparetly needed.

When I strum you, I try and
Channel all of the souls that
Knew you before me.

The memories and
Unheard melodies.
Snapshots frozen in time.

Waiting for someone to set
A flame to your frame and release
Everything trapped inside of you.

I acknowledge that the music
I play through you is a collaboration
With the many that came before me.

<u>Downpour</u>
When I discovered that water holds
Memory, I realized that raindrops
Are simply the moments when
Two people fall in love for the first time.
Their love falling through the sky and
Hurdling towards the ground beneath.
Nourishing the soil and saturating the
Earth with love, compassion, and joy.
If only we'd be so lucky to get caught
In a downpour.

<u>Mockingbird</u>
When I glanced out my window
I noticed the most spectacular bird.
I waited for it to sing a beautiful song,
But was caught off guard when instead it
Sang me a dark and melancholy ballad.
When I asked it what kind of bird it was
It told me it was a mockingbird.

<u>Windows</u>
One day I hope there is a
Museum exhibit of my life,
Displaying a curation of
Moments viewed from the
Frames of my bedroom
Windows.

Pillowy snowflakes dusting
The tops of pine trees.

A sleepy cat basking in the
Rays of the afternoon sun.

Headlights of a car leaving
In the middle of the night.

My wife watching the rain
Pour, and the lightning strike.

Browning plants begging
Me to water them.

Waves crashing through
The reef break.

SHELBY C. BACUS

A sunrise, and a final
Sunset.

Idyllic frames of serenity and joy,
Perfectly captured in a 4x4 frame.

<u>Power lines</u>
Grounding the chaos and
Tethering a life source.
Connecting the flow of
Energy from one to another.

<u>Oversaturated</u>
I feel so saturated with
Your love that I couldn't
Absorb more if I tried.

<u>Less</u>
I remind myself that
The less I have, the
More I have to strive for.
When you have it all,
What do you live for?

<u>Simple things</u>
Taking photos of my
Dog while he's sleeping.

Listening to music
On a record player.

The first sip of coffee
After a rough night.

Kisses on a warm
Sunday morning.

That time my dad and I
Spent five minutes looking
At a cool cloud in the sky
Without a care in the world.

<u>Too much</u>
All I wanted to do
Was text you that
I was thinking of you.

To let you know that
You were on my mind.
To remind you that
I was missing you.

But instead I sent you
A text saying "how's it going?"

Impersonal,
Detached, and
Riskless.

How do I learn to say
What I am feeling to

The people I care about
Without the overwhelming

Feeling that I
Am being "too much"?

<u>Patches</u>
My heart is covered
In beautiful patches.
A reminder of the many
Who mended my heart
Back together after it
Had been torn to pieces.

<u>Sea glass</u>
I have to remind myself that
Sometimes something that
Started out broken, can be
Shaped into something beautiful.

<u>Confessional</u>
I'm not actually bad
At doing laundry...
I just love the joy it
Brings you whenever I
"Accidentally" shrink
My sweaters to a size
Too small for me, but
A perfect fit for you.

<u>Weeds</u>
If only we could
Spread kindness as
Quick as a dandelion
Spreads its seed.
A weed that could
Cover the planet.

<u>Little details</u>
I memorized your coffee order
The first time I watched
You order it, so that I could
Surprise you with coffee on
Our very first date.

<u>Enlightenment</u>
When you can't tell
Where the ocean ends
And the night sky begins.
Both everything and
Nothing all at once.

<u>Cold feet</u>
Love is when you don't hesitate
To wrap me in your arms when I get
Into bed after a long cold night.
Always sacrificing your warm body
To breathe life back into mine.

<u>Caught in your arms</u>
When I feel myself straying
I feel your hands guiding
Me back to safety.

When I get cold at night
You don't hesitate to wrap
Me in your arms.

When my eyes start closing
During the movie we picked out
My head fits perfectly on your shoulder.

Your touch has always been
A light in the darkest of rooms.

Acknowledgements

This collection of poetry would not have been possible, if I had never stepped through the door of my therapist's office. By learning to share my life story with a complete stranger, I began to understand what being vulnerable truly meant. When I struggled with finding the words to describe what I was feeling, she always encouraged me to express myself through writing. For that, I am forever grateful. And to those that took the time to read my poetry before it had been published, it has never gone unnoticed. Thank you for your support. Remember to always be humble and kind.

<u>About the Author</u>

The author Shelby C. Bacus, first began writing this collection of poetry while living on a fishing trawler conducting research on the Bering Sea. She wrote this book while finishing the final year of her PhD in Marine Biology from the University of Alaska Fairbanks (something she would strongly advise against trying to do simultaneously). While living in Kodiak, Alaska, she credits the beauty of her surroundings and the warmth of her community for much of her writing inspiration.

When she isn't writing, she enjoys spending time exploring the outdoors with her dog Mateo, volunteer firefighting, curating playlists on Spotify, cooking for her friends, listening to audiobooks, playing the guitar, and selling baked goods at the farmers market during the summer. She thinks that the simple pleasures in life include a good cup of coffee, mountain sunrises, taking photos of her dog while he is sleeping, the smell of baking bread, vinyl records, and making others smile. If anything, she hopes that this book of poetry makes you smile.

www.ingramcontent.com/pod-product-compliance
Lightning Source LLC
Chambersburg PA
CBHW041455010526
44107CB00014B/1044